Table of Conte

Short Read 1 • Realistic Fiction

Read the passage. Then answer questions 1–10.

The Storm

1 A loud crash woke Anna from her dream. One minute she was flying over the schoolyard, swooping and gliding high in the air, hearing the wind rush by. The next minute, she was wide awake in the dark, wondering why her bed felt so hard. Then Anna remembered: She wasn't in her bed or even in her bedroom. She was in a sleeping bag in a little tent in the woods at Pine Tree State Park. She was on her first camping trip at last.

2 When the next crash came, Anna jumped. She heard Dad roll over. Anna peered out of the open tent flap. The sky was dark, and branches rustled in the wind. Rain was on the way; it was going to be a thunderstorm! Mom sat up and said, "Lucky you! Your very first camping trip, and you'll see a storm in the woods!"

3 "Will we get wet?" Anna asked as she grabbed her mother's hand. "Will the thunder hurt us?"

4 "No, we're camped in a good, safe spot," Dad said, "and our tent will keep us nice and dry."

continued

5 A few raindrops began to patter softly on the leaves. It was a cozy sound, and Anna relaxed. Then suddenly came another peal of thunder, and the rain changed to a steady downpour. Mom held a flashlight while Anna helped Dad zip the tent flap closed. "Let's talk about what we'll do tomorrow after the rain," Dad suggested. They lay in the dark tent and talked as the rain and the wind swirled around them. Anna suggested many ideas and nearly forgot about the storm until a flash of lightning lit up the tent. It was bright enough to see everything: Mom, Dad, and their sneakers and backpacks.

6 "Oh no, I forgot about lightning!" wailed Anna.

7 "There's nothing to worry about, Anna," Mom said. "The lightning is far away from us, even though it lights up our tent."

8 "How do you know? Are you just saying that to make me feel better?" Anna asked fearfully.

9 "No, it's really true. You can tell by the timing. A boom of thunder always comes after a flash of lightning. If they're close together, the storm is close by. If they're more than a few seconds apart, the storm is more distant."

10 Just then another flash of lightning lit up the tent. Mom, Dad, and Anna counted together: "One . . . two . . . three . . . four . . . five." On the count of six, they heard a rumble of thunder.

11 "Five seconds between the lightning and thunder," said Mom. "That means the storm is about one mile away. We can see it and hear it, but it's pretty far from us."

12 "Thank goodness for that," said Anna.

13 "Mother Nature is putting on a show," said Dad. "Tomorrow is the Fourth of July, but we're having our own special fireworks display right now."

14 Anna listened to the rain tapping softly on the tent. It was cozy in her sleeping bag, lying close to her parents. Before long, she was asleep.

continued

1. This question has two parts. Answer Part A first. Then answer Part B.

Part A How does Anna feel when she first notices the storm?

A determined

B calm

C amused

D worried

Part B Which sentence from the passage best supports the answer to Part A?

A A loud crash woke Anna from her dream.

B "Will we get wet?" Anna asked as she grabbed her mother's hand.

C The next minute, she was wide awake in the dark, wondering why her bed was so hard.

D It was cozy in her sleeping bag, lying close to her parents.

2. Dad's use of the words "Mother Nature" shows that he thinks of nature and the outdoors as—

A friendly.

B dangerous.

C sneaky.

D mysterious.

3. Read this sentence from the passage.

Tomorrow is the Fourth of July, but we're having our own special fireworks display right now.

Why does Dad mention a fireworks display?

A to compare fireworks to a camping trip

B to show that fireworks are the same as lightning

C to suggest something to do tomorrow

D to help Anna see that lightning can be beautiful

continued

4. This question has two parts. Answer Part A first. Then answer Part B.

Part A How does Anna feel at the end of the passage?

A calm

B excited

C nervous

D sad

Part B Which detail from the passage best supports the answer to Part A?

A The storm is far away.

B Anna is tired and wet.

C Anna goes to sleep.

D A storm wakes Anna up.

5. What can you tell from the illustration? Choose each detail you can learn from the illustration. Check the box next to each detail you choose.

- ☐ The family enjoys their camping trip.
- ☐ Anna has never been camping before.
- ☐ Camping in the rain isn't any fun.
- ☐ Mom and Dad like to camp near other families.
- ☐ Dad cooks dinner over a campfire.
- ☐ Anna is afraid of thunderstorms.
- ☐ Anna helps set up the tent.

6. Think about how Anna feels at different points in the story. Choose the feeling word that matches each sentence from the passage. Write the word next to the correct sentence.

safe	**happy**	**excited**	**scared**

Details	**Feelings**
She was on a camping trip at last!	
They lay in the dark tent and talked while the rain and the wind swirled around them.	
"Oh no, I forgot about lightning!" wailed Anna.	
It was cozy in her sleeping bag, lying close to her parents.	

continued

7. Which four details should go in a retelling of this passage? Choose the four details and number them in the correct order.

___ It is the Fourth of July.

___ A lightning flash lights up the tent and frightens Anna.

___ Anna flies over the schoolyard.

___ Mom explains how to tell if a storm is near or far away.

___ Anna wakes up in a tent during the night.

___ The family puts their backpacks and sneakers in the tent.

___ Dad is excited about seeing fireworks.

___ The sound of rain lulls Anna to sleep.

8. Why do Mom, Dad, and Anna count out loud? Use details from the passage to support your answer.

9. How do Mom and Dad try to help Anna feel safe? Use details from the passage to tell what they do.

continued

10. How does Anna's view of the storm differ from the way Mom and Dad view it? Use four or more details from the passage to support your answer.

Short Read 2 • Adventure

Read the passage. Then answer questions 1–10.

Going Home

1 Malia waited by the big elm tree that morning. The horse was there again, munching on the tall green grass. His coat shone in the morning sun and his long mane rustled in the breeze. He was the most beautiful creature Malia had ever seen.

2 Her heart racing, Malia moved slowly toward him. She spoke in a low voice. "That's a good boy, Pega. Remember me? I'm your friend."

3 She clutched a rope in one hand. In the other, she held a sack with bread and crisp green apples. Pega's ears twitched as she approached, and one large brown eye regarded her, but he kept eating. The first time she had tried to approach him all those weeks ago, he had run off. Now, though, he just watched her.

4 Birds called in the trees. From behind her at the farm came a loud yell. Mr. Brandt was yelling at one of the workers again; he was a cruel man.

continued

5 Pega raised his head when Malia stopped next to him. His soft white mouth wiggled. She smiled and pulled an apple out of the bag. Pega took it from her hand, his white teeth nearly as large as her fingers. As he munched on the apple, his whiskers moved up and down. Moving slowly, Malia removed the rope from the bag and draped it over his neck. Then she knotted her fingers in his coarse mane and hopped up onto his back.

6 The horse froze, startled. She feared that he might throw her off and run away, as he had done before. Instead, he relaxed after a moment. Malia sat there shaking, her breath uneven and her vision clouding. A tear slipped down her cheek.

7 "Thank you!" she whispered fiercely.

8 Today had to be the day. She could not wait any longer. Her family was back in Virginia, miles and miles away—too far to walk for someone as small as she was. Riding Pega home was her only chance. Even then the trip would be risky.

9 She tugged the rope to the left and nudged Pega's sides with her feet. He started unsurely and then began trotting through the meadow, following a game trail.

10 "That's a good boy, Pega!" She had named him "Pegasus" after the old story about a winged horse that flew through the sky like a bird. The name was a good omen. He would carry her home. She just knew it.

11 She rode for hours through the thick forest. Malia's fear grew as the sun rose higher. Mr. Brandt would know by now that she was missing, and he would come after her.

12 Mr. Brandt had come to her family's cabin six months ago, looking for workers to hire for his farm. The pay he promised was good, and he claimed that the work was easy. Malia's parents were poor. Their harvest had failed, and they needed the money. Even though Malia was only ten years old, she had left with Mr. Brandt. She and the other workers he hired traveled many miles to his farm.

13 There she labored all day, every day. She fed the chickens, cared for the horses, and helped in the fields. The work was hard, and Mr. Brandt did not pay her. He was an angry man who treated everyone badly. She was afraid of him, and the thought of staying any longer made her stomach shrivel into a small, tight knot.

14 Malia's parents were freed slaves. They spoke proudly of how they had bought their freedom from their old master. They had been free a long time, Malia knew, and she was not going to be anyone's slave.

15 That night, as she and Pegasus hid in a stand of young trees, a group of men came crashing through the forest. She recognized Mr. Brandt's voice when they paused nearby. "We have to find her before she makes it to the main road," he said. "I can't afford to lose another worker."

16 Their torches danced through the trees. Dogs barked in the distance. She heard the men discussing tracks and arguing over what direction they led. When they moved on, Malia started breathing again.

17 She and Pega traveled two more days through the forest. They saw a wolf eating its dinner. A snake hissed at them from on top of a rock. Deer watched with upright ears and large brown eyes before bounding off.

18 Finally, they came to the road. Looking down the road, Malia recognized the hills far off. She felt so grateful that tears came to her eyes. On the other side of those hills was her home. Together, she and Pega set off to find it.

continued

1. Read these sentences from the passage.

> Her heart racing, Malia moved slowly toward him. She spoke in a low voice. "That's a good boy, Pega. Remember me? I'm your friend."

Why does Malia move and speak to Pega in this way?

A She wants to show that she is his master.

B She does not want to frighten him.

C She is afraid that he will attack her.

D She fears that he will think she is someone else.

2. This question has two parts. Answer Part A first. Then answer Part B.

Part A How does Mr. Brandt act toward the workers on his farm?

A He pays them fairly if they work hard.

B He treats his workers poorly.

C He gives them work that is easy to do.

D He allows them to buy their freedom.

Part B Which details from the passage support the answer to Part A? Check the box next to each detail you choose.

- ☐ Mr. Brandt does not pay the workers as promised.
- ☐ Mr. Brandt hires workers from far away.
- ☐ Mr. Brandt makes his workers work every day.
- ☐ Mr. Brandt encourages the workers to ride his horses.
- ☐ Mr. Brandt does not want to lose another worker.

3. This question has two parts. Answer Part A first. Then answer Part B.

Part A Read this sentence from the passage.

> She was afraid of him, and the thought of staying any longer made her stomach shrivel into a small, tight knot.

What is the meaning of the word shrivel?

A grow

B shrink

C drop

D shine

Part B Which phrase from the sentence **best** helps you understand the meaning of shrivel?

A afraid of him

B the thought of staying

C any longer

D small, tight

continued

4. As Malia and Pega travel through the forest, Malia remembers how she had been hired by Mr. Brandt.

What purpose does this information serve in the story?

A It explains how Malia came to live at Mr. Brandt's farm.

B It tells why Mr. Brandt always yells at his workers.

C It shows that Malia does not understand Mr. Brandt.

D It helps the reader see why Pega likes Malia.

5. Identify the sentences that show the narrator's point of view and the sentences that show Malia's point of view. Write a "1" next to the sentences that show the narrator's point of view, and write a "2" next to the sentences that show Malia's point of view.

___ He was the most beautiful creature Malia had ever seen.

___ Mr. Brandt was yelling at one of the workers again; he was a cruel man.

___ His long mane rustled in the breeze.

___ "Thank you!" she whispered fiercely.

___ She feared that he might throw her off and run away, as he had done before.

___ Their torches danced through the trees.

___ Looking down the road, Malia recognized the hills far off.

6. Which word **best** describes how Malia feels at each point in the story? Choose the feeling word that matches each sentence from the passage. Write the word in the correct box.

nervous	**hopeful**	**surprised**	**determined**
angry	**relieved**	**frightened**	

Details	Feelings
Her heart racing, Malia moved slowly toward him.	
"Thank you!" she whispered fiercely.	
They had been free a long time, Malia knew, and she was not going to be anyone's slave.	
On the other side of those hills was her home.	

continued

7. Choose the events that took place in Malia's life before the beginning of this story. Check the box next to each event you choose.

- ☐ Pega trotted through a meadow, following a game trail.
- ☐ Malia was thrown off Pega when she tried to ride him.
- ☐ Mr. Brandt went to Malia's home looking for workers to hire.
- ☐ A snake hissed at Malia and Pega.
- ☐ Several men went out to search for Malia.

8. Why did Malia name the horse "Pega"? Use details from the passage to explain.

9. What can you tell about Malia from the way she handles Pega? Give at least two details from the text to support your answer.

continued

10. How and why does Malia escape from the farm? Use four or more details from the passage in your answer.

Short Read 3 • Legend

Read the passage. Then answer questions 1–10.

Rabbit Shoots the Sun

1 Long ago, Rabbit was a brave creature, unafraid of anyone. He was also quarrelsome. Rabbit enjoyed arguing with anyone who didn't do as he liked.

2 One time, Sun was behaving badly. For weeks, Sun created heat so intense that the animals became weak. When a rain cloud approached, Sun shooed it away. Sun enjoyed being so powerful.

3 Rabbit, along with the other animals, suffered mightily. All the plants he liked to eat had died. Also, Sun was drying up the streams and ponds. Soon there would be no water or food left.

4 He cried, "Sun, stop this nonsense! You are making us all suffer. Stop this heat and let the clouds come and rain over the land."

5 Sun just laughed and shone even hotter.

continued

6 "Sun has to be taken down a peg or two!" Rabbit said. "Someone has to teach her a lesson, and I'm just the one to do it."

7 So the next morning, Rabbit got a bow and arrow and waited in the spot where Sun rose each day. He would shoot Sun to make her stop shining so much.

8 However, Sun had heard Rabbit's threats. Instead of coming up at the usual spot, Sun rose in a different place. When Sun appeared that next morning, the arrow missed her by a mile. Higher in the sky, the arrows couldn't reach her.

9 Sun shone even brighter, her angry rays beaming down on the earth. It was another horribly hot day.

10 The next morning, Rabbit was weak. Still, he got up before dawn to shoot Sun. However, Sun rose quicker than usual, and Rabbit got his arrow off one second too late.

11 The next morning, Rabbit lay in wait again. This time, Sun was confident that Rabbit was too weak to hit her, and she rose slowly. But Rabbit's arrow pierced Sun's side, and liquid fire spewed from the wound.

12 The boiling liquid spilled onto the earth, setting everything afire. Animals ran in fear and hid in caves. Rabbit ran toward a cave, but the fire was almost upon him.

13 "Come and hide under me!" cried a green bush. "The fire will pass over me, and we won't be harmed."

14 So Rabbit hid under the bush until the fire passed by. When it was safe to come out, he noticed the top of the bush had turned golden. Today, we know this bush as the desert yellow brush.

15 The fire frightened Rabbit, and he was different from then on. He no longer challenged anyone. Today, he is fearful and timid, and he runs at the first sign of danger.

16 Sun changed a lot, too. Instead of showing off her power, now Sun shines just enough to warm the earth. She allows clouds to come and release their rain. However, Sun does rise slowly, peeking over the horizon for danger. Sun also shines so brightly that no one can look at her long enough to aim an arrow.

continued

1. This question has two parts. Answer Part A first. Then answer Part B.

Part A How does Rabbit feel about Sun at the beginning of the story?

A disappointed

B upset

C joyful

D amused

Part B Which detail from the passage supports the answer to Part A?

A Rabbit hides under a small green bush to get away from the fire.

B Rabbit becomes weaker and weaker, and needs water and food.

C Rabbit shoots an arrow at Sun, who burns the earth with liquid fire.

D Rabbit becomes frightened, and he stops challenging others.

2. Read this sentence from the passage.

> "Sun has to be taken down a peg or two!" Rabbit said.

What does the phrase taken down a peg or two mean?

A made to feel less pride

B hidden inside a closet

C moved to a different position in the sky

D hung on a hook

3. What does the illustration show about the story setting?

A how the land looks after fire falls from the sun

B how dry and wilted everything is

C the kinds of animals that are suffering

D what the lakes and streams look like

continued

4. This question has two parts. Answer Part A first. Then answer Part B. Read this sentence from the passage.

> But Rabbit's arrow pierced Sun's side, and liquid fire <u>spewed</u> from the wound.

Part A What is the meaning of <u>spewed</u>?

A poured out

B turned back

C shied away

D looked up

Part B Which word from the sentence in Part A helps you understand the meaning of <u>spewed</u>?

A arrow

B side

C wound

D liquid

5. Which words describe what Rabbit was like at the beginning of the story? Check the boxes next to the adjectives that describe Rabbit.

- ❑ timid
- ❑ brave
- ❑ angry
- ❑ quarrelsome
- ❑ frightening
- ❑ cruel

6. Which events belong in a retelling of this story? Choose five events and number the events in the correct order.

___ Rabbit told Sun to stop shining so much, but Sun refused.

___ Sun laughed at Rabbit.

___ After the fire, Rabbit became timid, and Sun warmed the earth.

___ Rabbit shot Sun with an arrow.

___ Liquid fire from Sun burned the earth.

___ The bush turned yellow on top.

___ Sun was shining so hot that animals and plants suffered.

___ Sun rose at a different place.

continued

7. How does Sun show her power in the story? Choose three sentences from the story that tell what Sun does. Check the box next to each sentence.

- ☐ For weeks, Sun created heat so intense that the animals became weak.
- ☐ One time, Sun was behaving badly.
- ☐ Also, Sun was drying up the streams and ponds.
- ☐ So the next morning, Rabbit got a bow and arrow and waited in the spot where Sun rose each day.
- ☐ Sun shone even brighter, her angry rays beaming down on the earth.
- ☐ However, Sun had heard Rabbit's threats.

8. How did Rabbit show that he was determined to solve the problem with Sun? Use details from the passage to support your answer.

____

____

____

____

____

____

9. How was Rabbit's point of view different from Sun's point of view? Use details from the passage to support your answer.

____

____

____

____

____

____

continued

10. What lessons does Rabbit learn in this story, and how does he learn them? Use three or more details from the passage to support your answer.

Short Read 4 • Drama

Read the passage. Then answer questions 1–10.

Rooster and the Comb of Fire

Cast of Characters

Griot 1

Griot 2

Rooster

Lion

Lioness

Cub

Note: A **griot** (gree-oh) is a traditional African storyteller.

Scene 1. Somewhere in the Forest

1 **Griot 1:** There was once a time in the forest when it was not Rooster who feared Lion, but Lion who feared Rooster.

2 **Griot 2:** It was Rooster with his crowing *(sound of drumming)* and his great red comb upon his head who made all the laws. *(longer drumming)* For all the animals believed that Rooster's red comb was a comb of fire. *(longer and louder drumming)*

3 **Rooster:** Bow down, bow down, for the red comb upon my head is a comb of fire.

4 **Griot 1:** Rooster even made a law for Lion. When Lion went out to hunt, it was the law that Lion should bring back a great number of fat and juicy bugs for Rooster to eat.

5 **Griot 2:** Rooster did not like the meat from Lion's hunt. He let Lion keep the meat for himself. Rooster liked only bugs.

continued

6 **Rooster:** Lion, I see you are going hunting. When you have killed your prey, you may keep the meat for yourself. But do not forget to catch a great many fat bugs for me.

7 **Lion:** I will not forget, Sir Rooster. I will have my meat, and you shall have your bugs.

8 **Rooster:** Do not forget or you will know the heat of the burning flame upon my head.

9 **Griot 1:** Now Rooster had tricked Lion and all the other animals of the forest into thinking that the bright red comb upon his head was a flickering fire.

10 **Lion:** *(returning from a hunt)* Rooster, I have caught a deer. And I have brought your juicy bugs, for I would not have you burn me with that flame upon your head.

11 **Rooster:** You are wise, Lion. You know your place. You know that I am ruler, and you are my servant.

12 **Griot 1:** Yes, my friends. In those days it was Rooster who was king and Lion was his servant.

13 **Griot 2:** Oh, how foolish was Lion! How sly was Rooster!

14 **Griot 1:** And that was the way for many years.

15 **Griot 2:** But one day it happened that Lion's family had no fire to warm their supper.

Scene 2. In Lion's Den

16 **Lioness:** Look, Husband, our fire has gone out. How shall we make a new one?

17 **Lion:** Perhaps I must go to Man and steal it in the night.

18 **Lioness:** No, I fear that is a great danger. Man is a clever thing and might catch you in his trap.

19 **Lion:** Where, then, shall we find fire?

20 **Cub:** Perhaps we might ask Rooster?

21 **Lion:** Rooster?

22 **Cub:** I could bring a sprig of short dry grass and ask that I might touch it to the flickering flame above his head.

23 **Lion:** Do you think Rooster would grant this?

24 **Lioness:** You have always been a good servant to him, Husband. We would not take away his flame, but only ask to light a spark.

25 **Lion:** Take with you some fat and juicy bugs to sweeten his generosity.

26 **Griot 1:** And so the young cub took the bugs and went to Rooster's hut.

Scene 3. In Rooster's Hut and Lion's Den

27 **Cub:** Rooster, good Rooster, are you at home? I have brought you bugs both fat and juicy.

28 **Griot 2:** But Rooster made no answer.

29 **Griot 1:** And so Cub took a step inside the door.

30 **Cub:** Rooster, good Rooster, are you at home? I have brought you bugs both fat and juicy.

31 **Griot 2:** Rooster was fast asleep and snoring loudly.

32 **Cub:** Rooster, awake, for I have brought you bugs both fat and juicy.

33 **Griot 1:** Rooster did not stir, but snored even louder.

34 **Cub:** Perhaps, if I touch my dry grass to the flickering flame upon his head, I will have my fire without needing to ask.

35 **Griot 2:** Cub went softly to Rooster's comb and set the grass against the brilliant red that glowed on Rooster's head.

36 **Griot 1:** But, of course, the grass did not light.

continued

37 **Cub:** What strange fire is this that does not burn?

38 **Griot 1:** And then with great daring . . .

39 **Griot 2:** He touched Rooster's comb.

40 **Cub:** This is no fire! This is no flame! What is this trick that Rooster has played?

41 **Griot 1:** Cub went home to his family.

42 **Cub:** Father, come see what I have found. Rooster has no flame upon his head, but only a fluttering red ruff. He has tricked us!

43 **Griot 2:** Lion went with Cub and they found Rooster still fast asleep.

44 **Cub:** Look, Father, there is no flame.

45 **Lion:** Rooster, Rooster, awake from your sleep. What is this trick you have played?

46 **Rooster:** Who wakes me from my lazy sleep? Lion, beware, or I will scorch you with this fire that glows upon my head.

47 **Lion:** Your trick is done, Rooster. I see through you. You have no fire, and you have no flame!

48 **Rooster:** Who told you this? Beware!

49 **Griot 1:** Then Lion grabbed Rooster by the comb upon his head.

50 **Rooster:** Now, Rooster, no more will we bring bugs for you. But you will become for every lion a tasty treat!

51 **Griot 1:** This is why . . .

52 **Griot 2:** . . . to this very day . . .

53 **Griot 1:** . . . Rooster lives with man . . .

54 **Griot 2:** . . . far away from Lion and his cubs . . .

55 **Griot 1:** . . . and Lion no longer fears Rooster with his comb of fire!

1. This question has two parts. Answer Part A first. Then answer Part B. Read this line from the play.

> I could bring a sprig of short dry grass and ask that I might touch it to the flickering flame above his head.

Part A What is the meaning of sprig?

A bright spark

B gentle tap

C red hat

D small branch

Part B Which phrase from the sentence in Part A helps you understand the meaning of sprig?

A above his head

B short dry grass

C might touch it

D flickering flame

continued

2. What can you tell from the illustration?

A Rooster and Lion were friends.

B The animals chose Rooster to be king.

C Many animals feared Rooster.

D Lion and Rooster were brothers.

3. This question has two parts. Answer Part A first. Then answer Part B.

Part A In the play, what is the role of Griot 1 and Griot 2?

A They make judgments about other characters.

B They provide food for Rooster.

C They find out how Rooster tricked Lion.

D They help Lion become king.

Part B Which line or lines from the play support the answer to Part A?

A Rooster did not like the meat from Lion's hunt. He let Lion keep the meat for himself.

B But one day it happened that Lion's family had no fire to warm their supper.

C Oh, how foolish was Lion! How sly was Rooster!

D Then Lion grabbed Rooster by the comb upon his head.

4. What is the central message of the play?

A The lion should be king of the animals.

B No one gets away with a lie forever.

C Roosters belong on farms, not in the forest.

D Animals should hunt for their own food.

5. Match each detail listed below with the correct scene in the play. Write the scene number (1, 2, or 3) in the box next to each detail.

Detail	Scene
Lion's fire goes out.	
Cub tries to light a fire.	
The setting is given.	
Rooster's secret is discovered.	
Cub enters Rooster's hut.	
Cub has a good idea.	
Main characters are introduced.	

continued

6. Which four words **best** describe the character of Rooster? Check the boxes next to the words that describe him.

- ❑ sly
- ❑ lazy
- ❑ forgetful
- ❑ foolish
- ❑ greedy
- ❑ fierce
- ❑ dishonest

7. How do the griots add to the reader's understanding or enjoyment of the story? Check the boxes next to the four things they do.

- ❑ They try to get fire from Rooster.
- ❑ They explain why Rooster makes all the laws.
- ❑ They help Lion find out Rooster's secret.
- ❑ They tell the setting.
- ❑ They bring fat and juicy bugs for Rooster.
- ❑ They describe the characters' actions.
- ❑ They tell what happens to Rooster after the story ends.

8. How does Rooster control Lion and the other animals of the forest? Use details from the play to support your answer.

____

____

____

____

____

____

9. In Scene 2, Lion and his family make a plan. Describe the plan and the reasons they think it will work.

____

____

____

____

____

____

continued

10. How would you describe the character of Cub? Choose at least two words to describe Cub and use details from the play to support your response.

Short Read 5 • Personal Narrative

Read the passage. Then answer questions 1–10.

Ox-Team Days on the Oregon Trail

(adapted excerpt from *Ox-Team Days on the Oregon Trail*, by Ezra Meeker, 1927)

1 We crossed the Missouri River on the 17th and 18th of May. The next day we made a short drive and camped within hearing of the steamboat whistle that sounded far over the prairie.

2 The whistle announced the arrival of a steamer. The steamer could carry a dozen or more wagons across the river at a time. A dozen or more trips could be made during the day, with as many more at night. Very soon we were overtaken by this throng of wagons. They gave us some troubles, and much discomfort.

3 The rush for the West was then at its height. The plan of action was to push ahead and make as big a day's drive as possible. So it is not to be wondered at that nearly all the thousand wagons that crossed the river after we did soon passed us.

4 "Now, just let them rush on. If we keep cool, we'll catch them before long," I told my companions.

continued

5 And we did. We passed many a team, broken down as a result of those first few days of rush. People often brought these and other ills upon themselves by their own foolishness.

Left on the Trail

6 Many folks did not go far before giving up the heavy loads. Soon we began to see abandoned property. First it might be a table or a cupboard, or perhaps a bed or a cookstove. Then feather beds, blankets, quilts, and pillows were seen. Very soon, here and there would be an abandoned wagon. Then we saw supplies like flour and bacon. All were left.

7 It was a case of help yourself if you would. No one would stop you. In some places a sign was posted: "Help yourself." Hundreds of wagons were left and hundreds of tons of goods. People seemed to vie with one another in giving away their things. There was no chance to sell, and they disliked to destroy their goods.

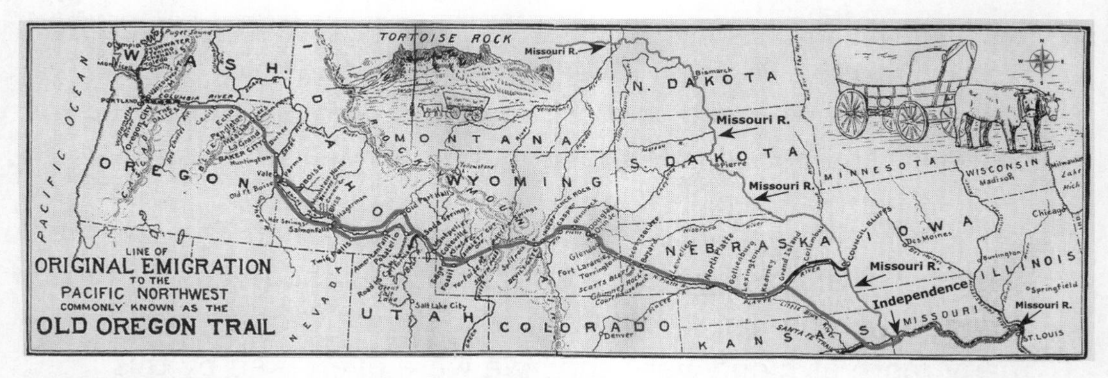

The bold line shows the Oregon Trail.

Ezra Meeker, the Pioneer

8 Ezra Meeker first went west in 1852, following the Oregon Trail. In the years that followed, thousands of other people did the same. Then in the late 1800s, railroads were built across the country. The trail was no longer needed, and it fell into disuse.

9 Meeker knew the trail was important to our nation's history. He wanted to make sure the trail was not forgotten. In the years after 1905, he made more trips on the trail. He talked to a lot of people and got towns and states to put up markers on the trail.

10 In 1978 the U.S. Congress gave the trail a new name. Now it is called the Oregon National Historic Trail. Today, the National Park Service cares for the trail. Cities, states, and private citizens help too. Thanks to them, you can still follow the route of the Oregon Trail by car and hiking.

continued

1. This question has two parts. Answer Part A first. Then answer Part B.

Part A Which sentence best states the main idea of the passage?

A Many people headed west on the Oregon Trail without knowing how hard it would be.

B Crossing the Missouri River on a steamboat gave wagons a good head start.

C It was easy to get supplies for the trip along the Oregon Trail by picking up things along the way.

D You couldn't lose your way on the Oregon Trail because it was very crowded.

Part B Check the boxes next to the sentences from the passage that support the answer to Part A.

- ☐ The whistle announced the arrival of a steamer.
- ☐ We passed many a team, broken down as a result of those first few days of rush.
- ☐ Many folks did not go far before giving up the heavy loads.
- ☐ Then we saw supplies like flour and bacon.
- ☐ Very soon we were overtaken by this throng of wagons.

2. Read these paragraphs from the passage.

> The rush for the West was then at its height. The plan of action was to push ahead and make as big a day's drive as possible. So it is not to be wondered at that nearly all the thousand wagons that crossed the river after we did soon passed us.
>
> "Now, just let them rush on. If we keep cool, we'll catch them before long," I told my companions.
>
> And we did. We passed many a team, broken down as a result of those first few days of rush. People often brought these and other ills upon themselves by their own foolishness.

In this text, how are the first and third paragraphs connected?

A These paragraphs compare the old wagons with the new wagons.

B These paragraphs state the main idea of the passage and give supporting details.

C The first paragraph gives the cause, and the third paragraph gives the effect.

D The first paragraph states a question, and the third paragraph gives the answer.

continued

3. Read these sentences from the passage.

> Very soon, here and there would be an abandoned wagon. Then we saw supplies like flour and bacon. All were left.

What is the meaning of the word abandoned?

A dirty

B thrown away

C rotten or spoiled

D old and broken

4. This question has two parts. Answer Part A first. Then answer Part B.

Part A What is the author's view of some travelers on the Oregon Trail?

A They did not bring enough supplies.

B They stole other people's goods.

C They had better plans of action than he did.

D They did not act with good sense.

Part B Which sentence from the passage **best** supports the answer to Part A?

A Soon we began to see abandoned property.

B People often brought these and other ills upon themselves by their own foolishness.

C It was a case of help yourself if you would.

D Very soon we were overtaken by this throng of wagons.

5. Below is a list of events described by the author, Ezra Meeker. Number them from 1 to 5 to show the order in which they happened.

___ He passed many broken-down wagons.

___ He saw furniture and supplies by the trail.

___ He crossed the Missouri River.

___ He was passed by a lot of wagons.

___ He heard the steamboat whistle.

6. What can you tell about Ezra Meeker from reading the text in the sidebar? Choose four details that describe the author. Place a check in the box next to each detail you choose.

☐ He succeeded in reaching the West.

☐ He was interested in history.

☐ He was the first pioneer to reach Oregon.

☐ He helped to preserve the Oregon Trail.

☐ He was born in 1852.

☐ He gave the trail a new name.

☐ The Oregon Trail was important to him.

continued

7. Based on the passage and the text in the sidebar, choose the cause of each effect listed. Draw a line connecting each cause to its effect.

Causes	**Effects**
The National Park Service takes care of the trail.	Towns and states put markers at points on the historic trail.
People pushed ahead too hard and too fast.	Travelers left belongings behind.
Loads were too heavy to haul.	The Oregon Trail was no longer used.
Railroads were built to connect the East and West.	Today, people can still drive or hike along the historic Oregon Trail.
A steamboat carried dozens of wagons across the Missouri River at a time.	Animals got hurt and teams broke down.
Ezra Meeker talked to people in towns along the trail.	The beginning of the trail was crowded.

8. Explain why there were tables, beds, and quilts along the Oregon Trail.

9. Look at the map. Did the author cross the Missouri River at the beginning, middle, or end of his trip? Tell how you know.

continued

10. In your view, did the author, Ezra Meeker, show that he had good judgment in this passage? Use four or more details from the passage to support your answer.

Short Read 6 • Biography

Read the passage. Then answer questions 1–10.

Norman Rockwell (1894–1978)

1 Norman Rockwell was one of America's best-known artists. During his long career, he produced many works of art for magazine covers. Some of his most famous covers were created for the *Saturday Evening Post*. That was a popular magazine for many years, and it helped Rockwell become known.

2 Rockwell always included real-life details in his work. His illustrations usually focused on everyday, small-town life, and they were often humorous. His painting called *Triple Self Portrait*, shown below, is a good example of his style.

continued

3 Rockwell began working as a freelance artist at just 17 years of age. He worked for numerous magazines at first. In 1916 he painted his first cover for the *Saturday Evening Post*. Over the next 47 years, he painted a total of 322 covers for the magazine. One such cover is *No Swimming*, shown below.

4 Rockwell also illustrated the official Boy Scout calendar for 50 years, from 1926 to 1976. During World War II, the Office of War Information gave out copies of his paintings called *Four Freedoms*.

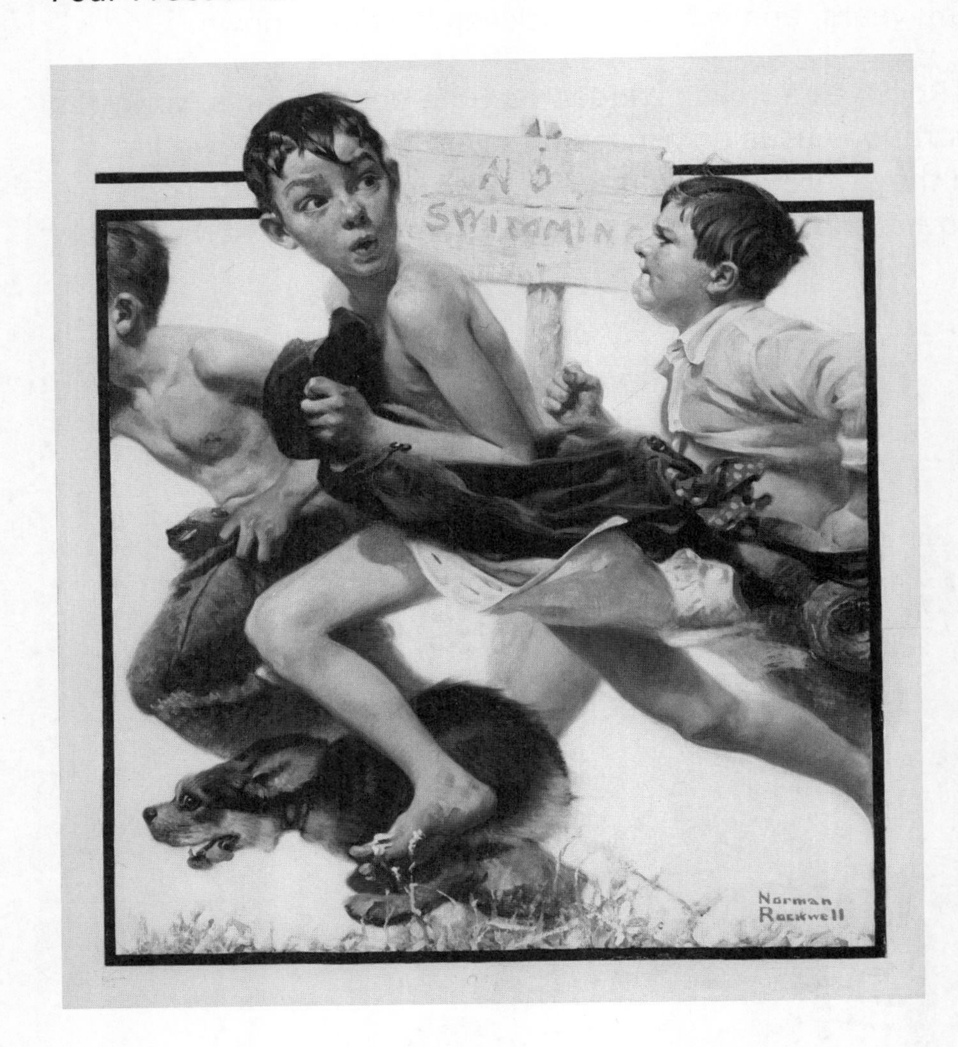

5 Later in life, Rockwell worked for *Look* magazine. He created work for the publication for 10 years. His pictures about the United States focused on things that were close to his heart, such as human rights. Rockwell painted *The Problem We All Live With* it after seeing Ruby Bridges being escorted to school on her first of school. Bridges was the first black student to attend a school in her neighborhood. Many people were against school integration. Rockwell's painting shows a young girl walking to school protected by police officers with the signs of protest around her.

6 Art critics were not kind to Rockwell. They called his work shallow. While Rockwell's paintings may not have required deep thought to understand, the public loved them. In 1977 President Ford gave Rockwell the Presidential Medal of Freedom to honor his life's work.

7 Rockwell married three times and had three sons. He died at the age of 84 after a long, fruitful life.

continued

1. Which sentence **best** states the author's view of Norman Rockwell?

A He became well known as a magazine artist but did not deserve the awards he got.

B He was the greatest American artist who ever lived.

C He created some good paintings, but most of his works were cheap magazine covers.

D He was not a great artist, but he was very popular.

2. What is the main focus of this passage?

A the life and work of artist Norman Rockwell

B magazine covers in the twentieth century

C how to become a freelance artist

D small-town life in the United States

3. This question has two parts. Answer Part A first. Then answer Part B.

Part A According to the passage, which event happened after Rockwell worked for *Look* magazine?

A He landed his first freelance magazine cover.

B He began illustrating the Boy Scout calendar.

C He painted *No Swimming*.

D He received the Presidential Medal of Freedom.

Part B Which paragraph gives details that support the answer to Part A?

A paragraph 1

B paragraph 3

C paragraph 5

D paragraph 6

continued

4. This question has two parts. Answer Part A first. Then answer Part B.

Part A Read this sentence from the passage.

They called his work shallow.

What does the word shallow mean as it is used in this sentence?

A mean and uncaring

B without deep meaning

C well liked and popular

D owned by the painter

Part B Which sentence from the passage helps you understand the meaning of shallow?

A Art critics were not kind to Rockwell.

B While Rockwell's paintings may not have required deep thought to understand, the public loved them.

C Rockwell always included real-life details in his work.

D His illustrations usually focused on everyday, small-town life, and they were often humorous.

5. Based on the pictures shown in this passage, which phrases **best** describe Rockwell's style? Check the box next to each phrase that describes Rockwell's style.

- ❑ lots of detail
- ❑ dull
- ❑ carefully drawn
- ❑ sometimes humorous
- ❑ true to life
- ❑ simple and beautiful
- ❑ cartoon-like

6. The author of this passage suggests that people liked Rockwell's paintings because they represent the American way of life. Choose two sentences from the passage that support this idea. Check the box next to each sentence you choose.

- ❑ Rockwell began working as a freelance artist at just 17 years of age.
- ❑ Rockwell also illustrated the official Boy Scout calendar for 50 years, from 1926 to 1976.
- ❑ During World War II, the Office of War Information gave out copies of his paintings called *Four Freedoms*.
- ❑ In 1916 he painted his first cover for the *Saturday Evening Post*.
- ❑ His painting called *Triple Self Portrait* is a good example of his style.

continued

7. The passage says that Rockwell's pictures focused on things that "were close to his heart." Based on the text and the pictures shown with this passage, choose four things that he cared deeply about. Check the box next to each thing Rockwell cared about.

— treating people fairly

— avoiding hard work

— being nice to your neighbors

— helping others

— leaving home

— breaking the law

— freedom

— winning at any cost

8. What text structure does the author use to present information in this passage? Explain how the paragraphs in the passage are connected.

9. How did Norman Rockwell become so well known throughout his career? Describe what he did to become well known.

continued

10. Look at the Rockwell painting called *Triple Self-Portrait*. Explain what the painting shows and what the title means.

Short Read 7 • Science Text

Read the passage. Then answer questions 1–10.

Why Is the Sky Blue?

(Passage excerpted from www.spaceplace.nasa.gov)

1 It is easy to see that the sky is blue. Have you ever wondered why? A lot of other smart people have too. And it took a long time to figure it out!

2 **The light from the sun looks white. But it is really made up of all the colors of the rainbow.**

3 A prism is a specially shaped crystal. When white light shines through a prism, the light is separated into all its colors.

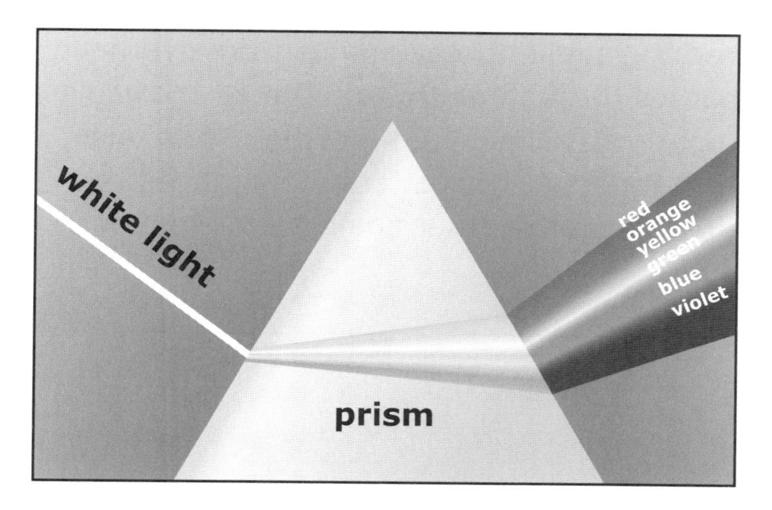

4 Like energy passing through the ocean, light energy travels in waves too. Some light travels in short, choppy waves. Other light travels in long, lazy waves. Blue light waves are shorter than red light waves.

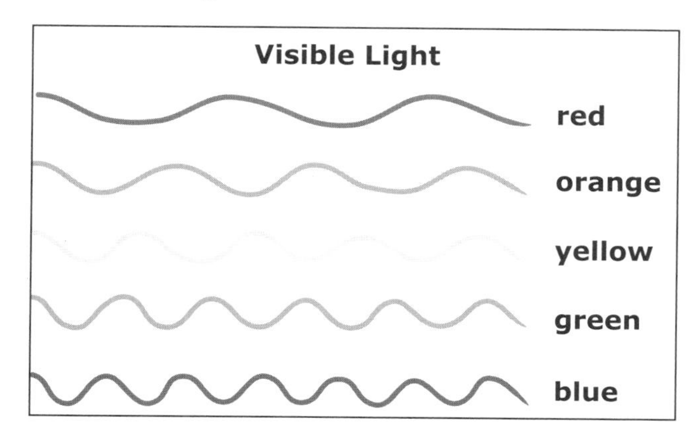

continued

All light travels in a straight line. That is, unless something—

- reflects it (like a mirror)
- bends it (like a prism)
- or scatters it.

5 So what scatters light? Sunlight reaches Earth's atmosphere and is scattered in all directions by all the gases and particles in the air. Blue light is scattered in all directions by the tiny molecules of air in Earth's atmosphere. Blue is scattered more than other colors because it travels as shorter, smaller waves. This is why we see a blue sky most of the time.

6 Closer to the horizon, the sky fades to a lighter blue or white. The sunlight reaching us from low in the sky passes through even more air than the sunlight reaching us from overhead. As the sunlight passes through all this air, the air molecules scatter the blue light many times in many directions. Also, the surface of Earth reflects and scatters the light. All this scattering mixes the colors together again so we see more white and less blue.

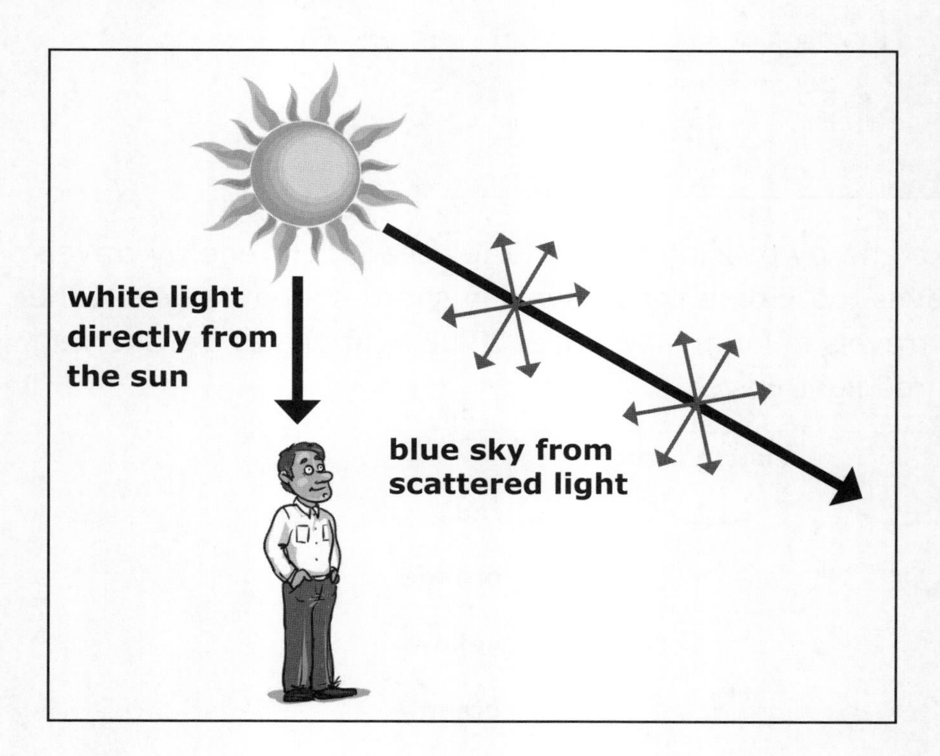

What Makes a Red Sunset?

7 As the sun gets lower in the sky, its light passes through more of the atmosphere to reach us. Even more of the blue light is scattered. This allows the reds and yellows to pass straight through to our eyes.

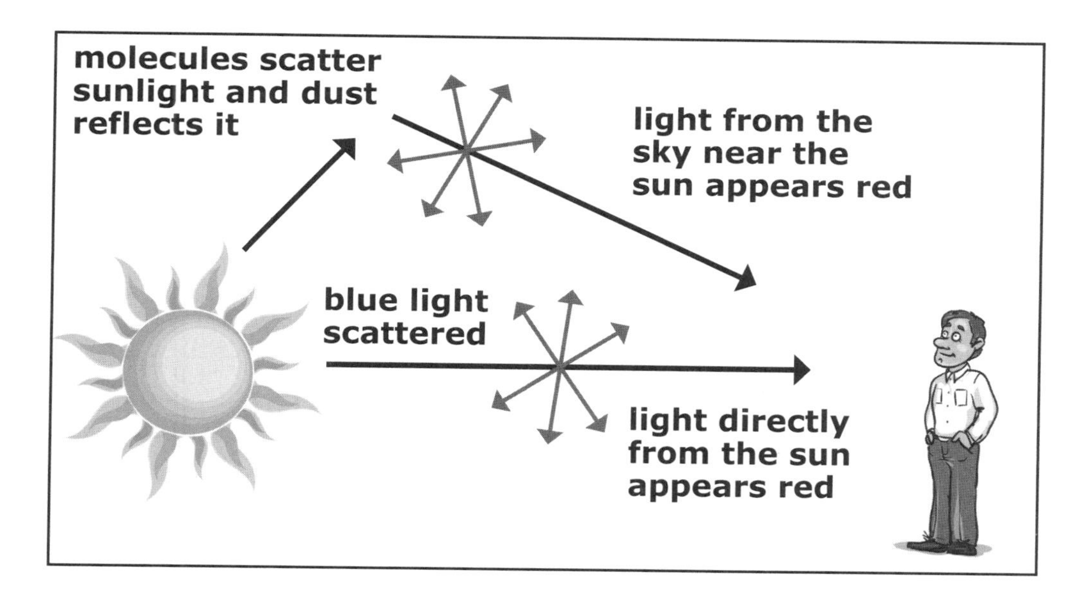

continued

1. Which sentence from the passage explains what a prism does?

A A prism is a specially shaped crystal.

B Like energy passing through the ocean, light energy travels in waves too.

C Sunlight reaches Earth's atmosphere and is scattered in all directions by all the gases and particles in the air.

D When white light shines through a prism, the light is separated into all its colors.

2. Read these sentences from the passage.

The light from the sun looks white. But it is really made up of all the colors of the rainbow.

Why does the author include these sentences in **bold** print?

A They give definitions for the hard words.

B They contain important information.

C They explain where you can find more information.

D They tell the reader what to read next.

3. This question has two parts. Answer Part A first. Then answer Part B. Read these sentences from the passage.

> Closer to the horizon, the sky fades to a lighter blue or white. The sunlight reaching us from low in the sky passes through even more air than the sunlight reaching us from overhead.

Part A What does the word horizon mean?

A the line where the sky and Earth seem to meet

B the highest point in the sky

C the surface of Earth

D the place that is farthest away from the sun

Part B Which detail from the sentences in Part A **best** helps you understand the meaning of horizon?

A the sunlight reaching us

B low in the sky

C passes through even more air

D sunlight reaching us from overhead

continued

4. This question has two parts. Answer Part A first. Then answer Part B.

Part A According to the passage, when is the sky **most likely** to look red?

A at noon

B when it hits a mirror

C at sunset

D in the middle of the night

Part B Choose two of the following sentences from the passage that support the answer to Part A.

A This is why we see a blue sky most of the time.

B Closer to the horizon, the sky fades to a lighter blue or white.

C All this scattering mixes the colors together again so we see more white and less blue.

D Even more of the blue light is scattered.

E This allows the reds and yellows to pass straight through to our eyes.

5. What can you learn from the illustration of **Visible Light**? Check the box next to each detail you choose.

- ❑ which color light travels in short waves
- ❑ which colors travel in longer waves
- ❑ which colors travel quickly
- ❑ which colors mix together
- ❑ which colors scatter

6. Look at the two illustrations of the man and the sun. Choose two things you can learn from these pictures. Check the boxes next to the two things you choose.

- ❑ how far away the sun needs to be to make a sunset
- ❑ why the sun sets near the horizon
- ❑ how dust and molecules scatter light
- ❑ why the blue light scatters more than other colors
- ❑ why we see red light at sunset

continued

7. The passage says that the sky looks blue because light from the sun scatters and the blue light scatters most. Choose three details from the passage that support this idea. Check the box to the left of each detail you choose.

   - ☐ The light from the sun looks white.
   - ☐ But it is really made up of all the colors of the rainbow.
   - ☐ Sunlight reaches Earth's atmosphere and is scattered in all directions by all the gases and particles in the air.
   - ☐ Blue is scattered more than other colors because it travels as shorter, smaller waves.
   - ☐ As the sun gets lower in the sky, its light passes through more of the atmosphere to reach us.
   - ☐ This allows the reds and yellows to pass straight through to our eyes.

8. Describe how light travels. Use details from the passage to support your answer.

____

____

____

____

____

____

9. How does the author feel about the subject of why the sky is blue? Tell how you know.

____

____

____

____

____

____

continued

10. In your own words, explain why the sky looks blue.

Short Read 8 • Technical Text/How-To

Read the passage. Then answer questions 1–10.

Sun Charts: The Secret to Great Gardens

1 Warm sunshine feels good! Sunlight gives your body vitamin D, so it is good for you, too. Still, too much sunlight can cause burns and even serious illness. It's important for people to get some sun, just not too much.

2 The same is true for plants. Plants are healthiest with just the right amount of sunlight. That's the biggest secret to having a great garden.

3 Would you like to plant a garden? Maybe you have a little space in your backyard. Maybe you'd like an indoor garden near a window in your home. Before you plant even one seed, do what successful gardeners do: Make a sun chart.

4 A sun chart shows you how much sun a place gets. This is called **sun exposure**. Different plants need different amounts of sun exposure. A sun chart will give you a head start on bringing your dream garden to life.

Prepare Your Chart

5 On a large sheet of paper, make a chart like the one shown below. Across the top, write the hours from 8 A.M. to 8 P.M. Then plan a day to complete the chart. Pick a nice, sunny day in the late spring or early summer. It should be a day when you are home near your garden spot most of the day.

8 A.M.	9 A.M.	10 A.M.	11 A.M.	12 P.M.	1 P.M.	2 P.M.	3 P.M.	4 P.M.	5 P.M.	6 P.M.	7 P.M.	8 P.M.

continued

Complete Your Chart

6 On your chart-making day, get up early! Around 8 o'clock, check your garden spot. Is the sun shining on it? Is it in the shade? Or is there a little of both, perhaps with some sun filtering through leaves? This is called **partial sun** or **partial shade**. Fill in the first box on your sun chart. Write "sun," "shade," "partial sun," or "partial shade."

7 Check the garden spot every hour and note the amount of sun. Keep careful notes on your chart. By 8 P.M., your chart will be complete.

8 Now look at your sun exposure chart. You've collected a lot of information! Count the number of hours of sunlight. Now you know how many hours of sunlight your garden will get each day. That will help you choose the best plants for your garden space.

Choose Your Plants

9 When you choose a plant, read the tag. When you choose seeds, read the package. You'll find out if the plant's needs for sun exposure match the conditions in your garden. Some plants need **full sun**. Some do best with **partial sun** or **partial shade**. Still others thrive in **shade** or **mostly shade**.

10 Have fun choosing the right kinds of plants for your garden spot. And have fun gardening!

More on Choosing Plants

11 First, make your sun exposure chart. Next, add up the hours of sunlight. You'll need to read each plant's tag, too. Then use this guide to choose your plants.

12 Your garden gets at least 6 hours of sun. Choose plants that need FULL SUN.

13 Your garden gets 3 to 6 hours of sunlight. Choose plants that need PARTIAL SUN or PARTIAL SHADE.

14 Your garden gets less than 3 hours of sun each day. Choose plants that need SHADE.

continued

1. This question has two parts. Answer Part A first. Then answer Part B.

Part A In paragraph 4, what is the meaning of the word exposure?

A mixing different things together

B the best way of doing something

C being out in the weather

D care and attention

Part B Which sentence from the passage helps you understand the meaning of exposure?

A That's the biggest secret to having a great garden.

B Maybe you have a little space in your backyard.

C Before you plant even one seed, do what successful gardeners do: Make a sun chart.

D A sun chart shows you how much sun a place gets.

2. Which sentence states the main idea of the passage?

A A sun chart will give you a head start on bringing your dream garden to life.

B Have fun choosing the right kinds of plants for your garden spot.

C It should be a day when you are home near your garden spot most of the day.

D On a large sheet of paper, make a chart like the one shown.

3. Based on the passage, what can you tell about the author's view of gardens?

A She dislikes indoor gardens.

B She likes shady gardens best.

C She thinks everyone should have a garden.

D She believes gardening is fun.

continued

4. This question has two parts. Answer Part A first. Then answer Part B.

Part A Based on information in the passage, how long does it take to fill in a sun chart?

A one morning

B about 12 hours

C about 24 hours

D one week

Part B Which part of the passage gives evidence for the answer to Part A?

A Prepare Your Chart

B Complete Your Chart

C Choose Your Plants

D More on Choosing Plants

5. Below is a list of steps for creating and using a sun chart. Number the steps in the correct order.

___ Choose plants that match the conditions in the garden.

___ Count up the hours of sunlight in the garden.

___ Record information in the chart.

___ Get some paper and prepare the chart.

___ Observe the garden, checking for sun and shade.

6. Choose three sentences from the passage that support the idea that sun charts can help you make a great garden. Check the box next to each sentence you choose.

- ❑ Different plants need different amounts of sun exposure.
- ❑ Warm sunshine feels good!
- ❑ On a large sheet of paper, make a chart like the one shown.
- ❑ Plants are healthiest with just the right amount of sunlight.
- ❑ Maybe you'd like an indoor garden, near a window in your home.
- ❑ You'll find out if the plant's needs for sun exposure match the conditions in your garden.

continued

7. Three friends want to plant gardens. Margo's garden gets 7 hours of sunlight each day. Brian's garden gets 1 hour of sunlight. Kim's garden gets 4 hours of sunlight. Use information from the passage and the sidebar to match each gardener to the type of plants he or she should plant. Match the plant type to the gardener.

Gardners	**Plant Tyes**
Margo	plants that need partial sun
Brian	plants that need full sun
Kim	plants that need shade

8. What information can you learn from a plant tag? Give at least two details.

____

____

____

____

____

____

9. What is the author's view of sun charts? Do you agree with the author's view? Why or why not? Explain.

____

____

____

____

____

____

continued

10. Explain how a sun chart can help a gardener. Support your answer with at least three details from the passage.

Short Read 9 • Fables

Read the passages. Then answer questions 1–10.

The Wolf and the Kid

by Aesop

1 There was once a little kid whose growing horns made him think he was a grown-up billy goat and able to take care of himself. So one evening when the flock started home from the pasture and his mother called, the kid paid no heed. He kept right on nibbling the grass. A little later when he lifted his head, the flock was gone.

2 The kid was all alone. The sun was sinking. Long shadows came creeping over the ground. A chilly wind came too, making scary noises in the grass. The kid shivered as he thought of the terrible wolf. He started wildly across the field, bleating for his mother. But halfway home, near a clump of trees, there was the wolf!

3 The kid knew there was little hope for him.

continued

4 "Please, Mr. Wolf," he said, "I know you are going to eat me. But first please play me a tune, for I want to dance and be merry as long as I can."

5 The wolf liked the idea of a little music before eating, so he struck up a merry tune. The kid leaped and frisked gaily.

6 Meanwhile, the flock was moving slowly homeward. In the still evening air, the wolf's piping carried far. The shepherd dogs pricked up their ears. They knew the song the wolf sings before a feast, and in a moment they were racing back to the pasture. The wolf ended his song suddenly and fled in fear. With the dogs at his heels, he called himself a fool for turning piper to please a kid.

7 *Do not let anything turn you from your purpose.*

The Fisherman and the Little Fish

by Aesop

1 A poor fisherman, who lived on the fish he caught, had bad luck one day and caught nothing but a very small fry. The Fisherman was about to put it in his basket when the little fish said:

2 "Please spare me, Mr. Fisherman! I am so small it is not worth carrying me home. When I am bigger, I shall make you a much better meal."

3 But the Fisherman quickly put the fish into his basket.

4 "How foolish I should be," he said, "to throw you back. However small you may be, you are better than nothing at all."

5 A *small gain is worth more than a large promise.*

continued

1. Read this sentence from "The Wolf and the Kid."

Do not let anything turn you from your purpose.

Why did the writer include this sentence?

A to explain the story's message

B to show that music and dancing are good

C to make fun of the wolf in the story

D to warn children to come when their mothers call

2. Read this sentence from "The Fisherman and the Little Fish."

A small gain is worth more than a large promise.

Which saying has the same meaning?

A All that glitters is not gold.

B Look before you leap.

C A bird in the hand is worth two in the bush.

D The early bird catches the worm.

3. This question has two parts. Answer Part A first. Then answer Part B.

Part A From the illustration, what can you tell about the fisherman?

A He caught a big basket full of fish.

B He caught something to eat.

C He wasn't happy until he caught a big fish.

D He set the little fish free.

Part B Which sentence from the passage **best** supports the answer to Part A?

A A poor fisherman, who lived on the fish he caught, had bad luck one day and caught nothing but a very small fry.

B "Please spare me, Mr. Fisherman!"

C "When I am bigger, I shall make you a much better meal."

D "However small you may be, you are better than nothing at all."

continued

4. This question has two parts. Answer Part A first. Then answer Part B. Read this sentence from the passage.

> The wolf liked the idea of a little music before eating, so he struck up a merry tune.

Part A What is the meaning of struck up in the sentence?

A attacked or hit

B lit on fire

C crashed into or knocked against

D began to play

Part B Choose two phrases from the sentence that help you understand the meaning of struck up.

A the wolf

B liked the idea

C a little music

D before eating

E a merry tune

5. Why did the kid ask Mr. Wolf to play a tune? Check the box next to each reason you choose.

- ❑ to delay the time when the wolf might eat him
- ❑ to have fun dancing
- ❑ to keep warm in the chilly wind
- ❑ to trick the wolf
- ❑ to make loud music that would bring the shepherd dogs
- ❑ to give the wolf a big appetite

6. Which five sentences should be included in a summary of "The Wolf and the Kid"? Choose the five sentences and number them in the correct order.

___ The wolf learned a lesson.

___ The kid was growing horns.

___ The kid paid no attention when it was time to leave the pasture.

___ The dogs heard the wolf's song.

___ The kid asked for a tune.

___ The sun went down.

___ The kid met the wolf.

continued

7. Choose four phrases from the passage that help readers feel the kid's fear. Check the box next to each phrase you choose.

- ❑ scary noises
- ❑ moving slowly homeward
- ❑ the terrible wolf
- ❑ the still evening air
- ❑ bleating for his mother
- ❑ leaped and frisked
- ❑ all alone

8. In your own words, retell the story of "The Fisherman and the Little Fish."

9. In these passages, the narrator says: "Do not let anything turn you from your purpose" and "A small gain is worth more than a large promise." Think about the wolf's actions. Does the narrator approve of what the wolf does? Support your answer with details from the passage.

continued

10. Compare and contrast the actions of the wolf and the fisherman. What did they want, what did they do, and what were the results? Use details from the passages to support your answer.

Short Read 10 • Poetry

Read the passages. Then answer questions 1–10.

Boats Sail on the Rivers

by Christina Rossetti

Boats sail on the rivers,
And ships sail on the seas;
But clouds that sail across the sky
Are prettier far than these.
5 There are bridges on the rivers,
As pretty as you please;
But the bow that bridges heaven,
And overtops the trees,
And builds a road from earth to sky,
10 Is prettier far than these.

continued

Is the Moon Tired?

by Christina Rossetti

Is the moon tired? She looks so pale
Within her misty veil:
She scales the sky from east to west,
And takes no rest.
5 Before the coming of the night
The moon shows papery white;
Before the dawning of the day
She fades away.

If All Were Rain and Never Sun

by Christina Rossetti

If all were rain and never sun,
  No bow could span the hill;
If all were sun and never rain,
  There'd be no rainbow still.

continued

1. What can you infer about the speaker (or poet) in these poems?

A She likes to observe the sky.

B She enjoys sailing.

C She is a weather forecaster.

D She often works by moonlight.

2. This question has two parts. Answer Part A first. Then answer Part B.

Part A In "Boats Sail on the Rivers," what is it that "builds a road from earth to sky"?

A a cloud

B a river

C a tree

D a rainbow

Part B Which of these gives the **best** clue to the answer to Part A?

A Boats sail on the water.

B The picture shows a rainbow.

C Bridges cross the river.

D The clouds are still pretty.

3. This question has two parts. Answer Part A first. Then answer Part B.

Part A Which sentence states the theme of "Boats Sail on the Rivers"?

A Things made by people cannot match nature's beauty.

B Some bridges are better than others.

C Our rivers and seas are too crowded with boats.

D Clouds make the best sailboats.

Part B Which line from the poem **best** supports the answer to Part A?

A But clouds that sail across the sky
Are prettier far than these.

B There are bridges on the rivers,
As pretty as you please;

C Boats sail on the rivers,

D And ships sail on the seas;

continued

4. In the poem "If All Were Rain and Never Sun," what is the meaning of the word span?

A to hide something by covering it

B to measure something

C to reach across something

D to climb to a high place

5. Choose two lessons or messages suggested in the poem "If All Were Rain and Never Sun." Check the boxes next to the answers you choose.

- ☐ We need all kinds of weather.
- ☐ If there is more rain, there will be bigger rainbows.
- ☐ Sunshine and rain are both good.
- ☐ Rainy days are sad.
- ☐ You don't need sun to make a rainbow.

6. In "Is the Moon Tired?" which details does the poet use to make the moon seem human? Check the boxes next to the three details that make the moon sound like a person.

- ☐ takes no rest
- ☐ from east to west
- ☐ looks so pale
- ☐ shows papery white
- ☐ the coming of the night
- ☐ before the dawning
- ☐ her misty veil

continued

7. The poet uses different pairs of rhyming words in these poems. Check the box next to each set of rhyming words on the list below.

- ☐ seas and these
- ☐ east and west
- ☐ rivers and heaven
- ☐ pale and veil
- ☐ sun and rain
- ☐ day and away
- ☐ night and white
- ☐ still and scales

8. In "Boats Sail on the Rivers," the poet compares clouds to ships and boats. Describe one way clouds are like ships and boats, and one way they are different, based on the poem.

9. How does the second stanza of "Is the Moon Tired?" build on the first stanza? Use details from the poem to support your response.

continued

10. Based on these three poems, how does the poet feel about nature? Use at least three details from the poems to support your response.

Short Read 11 • Social Studies Texts

Read the passages. Then answer questions 1–10.

The Great Mississippi

1 The Mississippi River is the greatest river in North America. Its name comes from a Native American group, the Ojibwa. They called it ***misi-sipi***, meaning "big river." In the 1800s, some people called it the "Father of Waters." The Mississippi begins at its source in Minnesota and ends in Louisiana. It is the longest river in the United States.

2 The actual length of the river changes, based on the amount of silt and erosion at its delta. As the river flows, it carries loads of soil and mud. The river dumps the mud at its mouth, or delta. So the length of the river changes as the mud piles up or flows away. Its length is usually about 2,350 miles.

3 At Lake Itasca, Minnesota, where the river begins, it is 20 to 30 feet wide. Its widest point is near Bena, Minnesota. There, it is more than 11 miles from one side to the other.

4 The river changes as it moves south. From its source to St. Paul, Minnesota, it is a clear stream. It meanders through the lowlands on a winding course. Lakes and marshes are common. From St. Paul to the mouth of the Missouri River, it is a huge, powerful river. It gathers streams and rivers from Minnesota, Wisconsin, Illinois, and Iowa. In St. Louis, the Mississippi joins the Missouri River. At this point, the river is often more than a mile and a half from bank to bank. Its water is often brown with mud. That is how it got another nickname, the "Big Muddy." Finally, as the river nears its end, it spills into the Gulf of Mexico.

5 The Mississippi River serves many purposes. Mainly, it is a source of fresh water. Millions of people depend on it, as do many kinds of animals. More than 200 species of animals live along the river. More than 260 species of fish live in the water. Nearly half of the nation's birds that migrate from place to place use the river along the way.

continued

6 For hundreds of years, people have used the river for travel. They also use it for shipping cargo—about 500 million tons each year! The cargo includes many important products, such as grain, coal, oil, and wood.

7 Farmers use water from the river to grow cotton, corn, soybeans, rice, and other crops. And every year, more than twelve million people visit the river. They boat, fish, and enjoy its beauty. These visitors create many jobs for people who live nearby.

The Mississippi River

Flooding on the Mississippi

1 From Minnesota to Louisiana, the Mississippi River flows about 2,350 miles. It is one of the world's most important waterways. Consequently, many cities, ports, and communities have developed along the banks of the river. Millions of people depend on the river for water and other uses. Farmers who live near the river produce huge quantities of grains and soybeans. Much of America's livestock is raised in this area.

2 Every year, the Mississippi overflows its banks and causes flooding. When people hear about the flooding, they think: DISASTER. It's on the news, it's on television, and it can cause serious problems.

3 Floodwaters can destroy farm crops. Farm animals get swept away. The water damages homes, schools, and businesses. People lose fresh drinking water, plumbing, and electricity. Some have lost their lives.

4 Floods can also destroy habitats. Wild animals have to flee to higher ground or drown. After the flood, the animals that survive may have trouble finding food. Paint, gasoline, and poisons enter the floodwaters and destroy both plants and fish. Coastlines can wash away.

5 While the flooding Mississippi is harmful to many, it is also a natural event. The Mississippi has flooded for thousands of years, and it will flood for thousands more. What many people ignore is that flooding is also good for the earth. It benefits animals, plants, and people.

6 One benefit of flooding is that it brings new life to the land. When floodwaters cover the land, they deposit rich topsoil. These rich deposits make the soil more fertile for growing crops. Some of the best farmland in the world lies along the banks of the Mississippi River.

continued

7 Another good result of flooding is wetlands, such as swamps, bogs, and marshes. These wetland areas provide habitats for fish, birds, and plants to live and thrive. They are an important part of the natural ecosystem.

8 Wetlands are important in two other ways. First, they actually help control floodwaters. Cities cannot absorb floodwater. But wetlands take in floodwater and store it. Water that flows into a wetland can gradually drain down into the soil. Wetlands also act as a kind of filter. They help clean floodwaters. Dirty or polluted water from a flood settles in wetlands. Then it seeps into the ground. As the water passes through the soil, it becomes cleaner.

9 While some floods carry tragedy, they can also carry promise. They create wetlands, enrich farmlands, and help all sorts of wildlife. Dirty or polluted water from a flood settles in wetlands. Then it seeps into the ground. As the water passes through the soil, it becomes cleaner.

10 While some floods carry tragedy, they can also carry promise. They create wetlands, enrich farmlands, and help all sorts of wildlife.

Mississippi River Facts

- The river formed from melting glaciers more than 10,000 years ago.
- Its depth varies from 3 to 200 feet.
- It is one mile wide in Alton, Illinois.
- More than 260 species of fish live in the river.

1. This question has two parts. Answer Part A first. Then answer Part B.

Part A According to "The Great Mississippi," how do silt and erosion affect the Mississippi River?

A They keep water from flowing into wetlands.

B They change the length of the river.

C They provide more habitats for fish.

D They reduce flooding by acting as levees.

Part B Which sentence from the passage **best** supports the answer to Part A?

A Its length is usually about 2,350 miles.

B So the length of the river changes as the mud piles up or flows away.

C As the river flows, it carries loads of soil and mud.

D At Lake Itasca, Minnesota, where the river begins, it is 20 to 30 feet wide.

2. What is the main idea of "The Great Mississippi"?

A The river's name came from the Ojibwa name "misi-sipi," meaning "big river."

B The Mississippi is the longest river in the United States.

C People have used the river for travel for hundreds of years.

D The Mississippi River serves many purposes for people and wildlife.

continued

3. What is the author's main point in "Flooding on the Mississippi"?

A Wetlands clean polluted water, provide homes to plants and animals, and reduce flooding on the Mississippi River.

B Flooding on the Mississippi River has happened for thousands of years, but most floods can be prevented.

C The Mississippi River floods every year because of heavy rains and the development of cities along its banks.

D Mississippi River floods can be harmful to people and animals, but they also have benefits.

4. This question has two parts. Answer Part A first. Then answer Part B. Read this sentence from "The Great Mississippi."

It meanders through the lowlands on a winding course.

Part A What does the word meanders mean?

A wanders here and there

B flows very fast

C joins with other streams

D moves toward the south

Part B Which phrase from the passage helps you understand the meaning of the word meanders?

A where the river begins

B its widest point

C a huge, powerful river

D on a winding course

5. Read this sentence from paragraph 1 of "Flooding on the Mississippi."

Consequently, many cities, ports, and communities have developed along the banks of the river.

Which phrase means about the same as consequently?

A for example

B on the other hand

C as a result

D in spite of this

6. What information about the river can you learn from the map in "The Great Mississippi"? Check the box next to each sentence you choose.

- ☐ It flows through 10 states.
- ☐ It supports many kinds of wildlife.
- ☐ Birds that migrate stop along the river.
- ☐ It ends in New Orleans.
- ☐ One of its nicknames is "Big Muddy."

continued

7. Read each piece of information in the chart. Decide whether the information is included in "The Great Mississippi" or "Flooding on the Mississippi." Put a check mark in the correct box beside each piece of information. If the information is included in both passages, put check marks in both boxes.

Information	The Great Mississippi	Flooding on the Mississippi
People and cargo travel up and down the Mississippi River.	❑	❑
Farms near the Mississippi River produce many crops.	❑	❑
Many people depend on the Mississippi River for water.	❑	❑
When the Mississippi River floods, it causes problems.	❑	❑
Floods on the Mississippi River help create wetlands.	❑	❑
Floodwaters help enrich the soil along the river.	❑	❑
The Mississippi River provides jobs for people who live near it.	❑	❑

8. In "Flooding on the Mississippi," what is the author's view of flooding? Is flooding good or bad? Use details from the passage to support your answer.

9. In "The Great Mississippi," how does the author present information in the first four paragraphs? Explain how the first four paragraphs are connected.

continued

10. How do humans and animals benefit from the Mississippi River? Use details from both passages to support your answer.

Short Read 12 • Science Texts

Read the passages. Then answer questions 1–10.

Can Plants Talk?

Fennel plant

What's unusual about the fennel plant?

Corn plant

Want to know more about how corn communicates?

Chili plant

Hey, chili plant, you're hot!

1 Some people talk to their plants. Some like to play music. They think it keeps plants happy and healthy. These ideas might seem a little daffy. But they just might be right.

2 Plants do not make noises we can hear. But scientists think that they can "talk." They don't speak words. But they send messages to other plants. They warn other plants of danger.

3 Some plants talk to one another with chemicals. For example, when a cabbage is cut or nibbled on, it gives off a gas to warn other cabbages. The message says something like, "A plant-eater is in the garden!" When the other cabbages sense the gas, they form a toxic chemical on their leaves. This poison says, "Stay away from me!"

4 We know that plants respond to light. They grow toward the light, or the sun. Now scientists have found that plants can make and hear sounds.

5 To test this idea, a team of scientists did an experiment with fennel plants. They know that fennel gives off chemicals that slow the growth of nearby plants. The plants will take less water and food from the soil so the fennel can get more.

continued

6 The scientists planted fennel next to chili plants. The chili plants grew slower than normal. Then the scientists did the same thing again with new plants. But this time they put the fennel inside a plastic box. The box kept the fennel's chemicals from reaching the chili plants. The results were amazing. The chili plants grew faster than ever!

7 The scientists believe the chili plants "knew" that fennel was nearby. How? They think the chili plants heard sounds from the fennel. The chili plants grew faster to protect themselves from the fennel's chemicals.

8 Another plant the scientists studied was corn. They know that the roots of young corn plants make clicking sounds. Sound waves travel easily through soil. The scientists wanted to know if other corn plants could hear these sounds. They wanted to test this idea. So they put the corn's roots in water. Then the scientists made clicking sounds. The roots moved toward the sounds! Scientists think the corn's clicking sounds warn other corn plants of danger. Maybe the young plants wanted to stay close to others.

9 So the next time you pass a plant, listen closely. It may not say hello. But it might be telling other plants about you!

Animal Talk

Sound

Coyotes howl and yip to talk to one another.

Humpback whales sing songs to talk to other whales.

Sight

A bee dances in the hive when it finds food so other bees will follow it to the food.

Fireflies light up their bodies to show where they are.

Touch

Chimpanzees greet one another by touching hands.

Dogs lick their pups to show them love.

Smell

Deer leave scents on tree branches and trunks to tell other deer to stay away.

Skunks let out a stinky odor to keep enemies away.

continued

1 Animals don't speak words like people, but they do "talk." They use sounds, sight, touch, and smell to let other animals know what they are thinking.

Dogs

2 A dog might bark when it wants to go outside or show that it is hungry. It might also mean that it wants your attention. A dog might even bark at other animals saying, "Stay away from me!" The bark turns into a growl when it's afraid. A whimpering dog may be saying many different things. The crying might say, "I hurt" or "I want that biscuit." It can also mean "Play with me" or "I'm glad to see you!"

3 Dogs also use their bodies to communicate. When a dog lowers its front legs to the ground and wags its tail, it wants to play. A dog might put its paw on your hand. Usually, that means the dog wants to be petted or get a treat. A happy dog will wag its tail. A dog may also wag its tail when it's scared. And if the fur rises up on its back, watch out. The dog is trying to look bigger to scare its enemy.

Whales

4 Whales sing to one another. Some songs tell other whales that it's time to hunt. Then they join together in a group and hunt schools, or groups, of smaller fish. Humpback whales sing songs to attract other whales. Parts of these songs repeat again and again. A song can last for 30 minutes!

5 Humpback whales also use their bodies to communicate. They might slap the water with their tails. Whales might breach, or jump out of the water, and then dive down. They also will swim fast toward another whale. They want to get the whale's attention or tell the whale something important.

Bats

6 Bats sing like birds, but the sounds they make are almost always too high for people to hear. Bats also have the ability to change the sounds they make to mean different things. If they are upset or afraid, their voices become squeaky and very high-pitched. Scientists compare bat singing to the way people talk. Bats can change their voices to make many different sounds, much like people. Also, each bat's sound is different from the sounds of others. That helps bats know who is singing.

7 So what are bats saying? They use sound to identify who and where they are. They also sing to tell a baby bat what to do. Sometimes, the bat makes a sound that warns other bats to stay away.

continued

1. This question has two parts. Answer Part A first. Then answer Part B.

Part A According to "Can Plants Talk?" what might make a cabbage give off gases?

A The cabbage hears a clicking sound.

B The cabbage sees a plant-eater.

C The cabbage gets cut or eaten.

D The cabbage senses a fennel plant.

Part B Which paragraph supports the answer to Part A?

A paragraph 2

B paragraph 3

C paragraph 4

D paragraph 5

2. This question has two parts. Answer Part A first. Then answer Part B. Read this sentence from "Animal Talk."

A whimpering dog may be saying many different things.

Part A What is the meaning of whimpering?

A scratching over and over

B making quiet whining sounds

C purring or grunting

D howling loudly

Part B Which phrase from the passage helps you understand the meaning of whimpering?

A bark at other animals

B turn into a growl

C when it's afraid

D the crying

continued

3. What important point is made in both "Can Plants Talk?" and "Animal Talk"?

A Plants are able to communicate with other plants and animals.

B All plants and animals use clicking sounds to send out warnings.

C Plants and animals cannot speak words, but they do send and get messages.

D Both plants and animals use sound, smell, sight, and touch to communicate.

4. According to "Animal Talk," which animals use smell to communicate?

A skunks and deer

B coyotes and bees

C whales and fireflies

D chimpanzees and dogs

5. In "Can Plants Talk?" what three steps did the scientists take to test whether corn plants respond to sound? Choose the steps and number them in the correct order.

___ They noticed that the corn plants moved toward the clicking sounds.

___ They put the roots of corn plants in water.

___ They put the corn plants inside a plastic box.

___ They made clicking sounds.

___ They played music for the corn plants.

___ They placed a fennel plant beside the corn plants.

6. "Animal Talk" says that animals can use body movements to communicate. Choose three details from the passage that support this idea. Check the box next to each detail you choose.

- ☐ A dog might bark when it wants to go outside or show that it is hungry.
- ☐ When a dog lowers its front legs to the ground and wags its tail, it wants to play.
- ☐ Some songs tell other whales that it's time to hunt.
- ☐ Whales might breach, or jump out of the water, and then dive down.
- ☐ Scientists compare bat singing to the way people talk.
- ☐ A dog may also wag its tail when it's scared.

continued

7. Look at the pictures in the passage "Can Plants Talk?" What information can you learn from the pictures? Check the two things you can learn.

- ❑ what a fennel plant smells like
- ❑ the sound corn plants make
- ❑ what a chili plant looks like
- ❑ the smell of chemicals from a cabbage
- ❑ the shape of a cabbage plant
- ❑ what a young corn plant looks like

8. According to "Animal Talk," why do bats sing? Give three reasons. Use details from the passage to support your answer.

____

____

____

____

____

____

9. What does the author of "Can Plants Talk?" think about the idea that plants can communicate? Do you agree with the author's view or not, and why?

____

____

____

____

____

____

continued

10. In what ways do animals and plants communicate? Use details from each passage to support your response.

Notes

continued

Notes

Notes

continued

Notes